# Collectible Locks

### An Illustrated Value Guide
### By Richard Holiner

COLLECTOR BOOKS
P.O. BOX 3009
Paducah, Kentucky 42001

R
683.32
H732
R-1

The locks illustrated in this book are from the collection of the author, Richard Holiner.

```
38212000926433
Main Adult
683.32 H732
Holiner, Richard
Collectible locks : an
illustrated value guide
```

Additional copies of this book may be ordered from:

COLLECTOR BOOKS
P.O. Box 3009
Paducah, Kentucky 42001

@ $5.95 Add $.50 postage for the first book &
$.20 for each additional book.

Copyright: Richard Holiner, 1979
ISBN: 0-89145-115-3

This book or any part thereof may not be reproduced
without the written consent of the Author and Publisher.

Printed by PURCHASE PRINTERS, Paducah, Kentucky

# Contents

| | |
|---|---|
| Lock History | 4 |
| Lock Terminology | 5 |
| Lock Facts | 7 |
| Lock Markings | 7 |
| Ward Locks, Wrought Iron | 8 |
| Ward Locks | 16 |
| Wafer, Scandinavian Type Jail Locks | 50 |
| Wafer Locks | 52 |
| 2 Lever Locks | 54 |
| 3 Lever Locks | 58 |
| 4 Lever Locks | 64 |
| 4 Lever, Railroad Pin Tumbler Locks | 66 |
| 4-, 5-, 6- Lever Push Key, Railroad Pin Tumbler Locks | 70 |
| 6 Lever Locks | 72 |
| 6 Lever Pancake Push Key Locks | 80 |
| 8 Lever Locks | 82 |
| Pin Tumbler Push Key Locks | 84 |
| Pin Tumbler Locks | 88 |
| Combination Locks | 96 |
| Vehicle Locks | 100 |
| Jail Lock | 104 |
| Safe Lock | 104 |
| Early Blacksmith Type Screw Key Locks | 106 |
| Oriental Locks | 108 |
| Worlds Fair Locks | 110 |
| Bank Vault Time Lock | 112 |

# Lock History

Possibly the oldest type of lock in existence is the wooden cross bar. It dates back to Egypt and other early biblical cities. The basic mechanical principle of the wooden cross bar is used in modern pin tumbler locks. The Ancient Romans were the first to actually make key-operated mechanical door locks. In the ancient city of Pompeii archaeologists uncovered a locksmith shop where they found many types of padlocks and door locks. Skewers and odd shaped prongs were also discovered. They were undoubtedly used as lock picks. The Etruscans in northern Italy are given credit for the invention of the ward lock. During the middle ages, warded locks were large and attractive in design. They were sometimes used to protect castles and monasteries. The ward lock was the most widely used from early times until the invention of the pin tumbler lock.

Locksmith guilds were formed during the middle ages. They regulated all forms of locksmithing from apprenticeship to the techniques of the masters. The guild regulations were followed until the nineteenth century. The lever tumbler was invented during the Renaissance. Combination locks, also called letter or number locks, were used in different stages of history but were never considered as secure locking devices until modern times when they were made into works of precision. Most early combination locks used letters and would open when turned to the correct word. The first true lock was constructed in the 1700's when an Englishman invented a lever tumbler lock that used more than one tumbler. From then on, locks became much improved in design and security. Rivalry for a better lock led to the greatest improvement in locks in over three thousand years.

The two most famous names connected to nineteenth century American lock history are Yale and Sargent. Lynus Yale was the inventor of the pin tumbler cylinder lock during the middle 1800's. His son improved upon his design so that it could be mass produced. James Sargent is associated with the development of time locks and was the first to make a practical specimen. Shortly after the first World War, locks that could withstand excessive vibrations were developed. During the early 1900's two remarkable inventions came forth. The first was invented by Harry Gussman in 1909--the key duplicating machine which ended hand filing and made for accurate reproduction of keys. In 1926 the Independent Lock Company developed the code machine which enabled them to make keys for locks according to their several numbers. This has especially benefited automotive locksmithing. Many more inventions have come to us in recent years. Of these, tools to measure tumblers without the disassembly of the locks and devices to open locks in emergency are the most notable.

# Lock Terminology

**Barrel Key** - One with a hole drilled in the stem.

**Bolt** - The part of a lock which is moved back and forth to create a locked or unlocked position when the key is turned.

**Cap** - The removable part of a lock which holds the tumblers and springs.

**Case** - The outside container for the bolt and other outside mechanism.

**Changes** - This term is used in place of the word "combination" for locks for the warded type.

**Change Key** - A key made to operate one particular lock.

**Codes** - A series of numbers by which a finished key can be made to a lock. More often, showing the lock number and corresponding combination.

**Combination Lock** - A lock using disc tumblers operated by a dial. Such locks do not use a key but are opened when the correct series of numbers are used.

**Cylinder Lock** - The complete mechanism of both cylinder and plug put together with tumblers which operate with a key.

**Dead Bolt** - A bolt which can be moved in either direction by the key but cannot be pushed back by any other means than the key when in the locked position.

**Disc Tumbler** - Tumblers used in combination locks. Made with a slot in the edge into which the bolts drop when all tumblers are brought into line by turning the dial.

**Dog** - Referred to as a stop on the bolt which prevents the bolt being thrown unless the correct key is used.

**Double Pitted Key** - Uses a blade on both sides of the barrel or stem.

**Drill Pin** - A pin projecting from the back plate of a lock and fits into the hole in the end of a barrel key.

**Flat Key** - A key made of sheet metal usually by the stamping process.

**Follower** - Used to hold the upper pins in place when a plug is taken out of a cylinder lock.

**Grand Master Lock** - A key that will open any lock in a large group of locks.

**Latch** - A lock with a beveled bolt that engages automatically when the door is closed.

**Lever Lock** - A flat piece of brass or steel swiveled on one end and cut on the other. This is the portion of the lock that the stop passes through.

**Master Keying** - Although a different key is used for each lock, the master key will open any of them.

**Paracentring Lock** - Cylinder type lock which uses a plug containing either wafer or pin tumblers which moves a bolt or other locking device by turning the plug with a key.

**Pin Tumbler** - A small bar moved by a key. Two or more are used in each hole of a pin tumbler lock and must divide before the plug will turn by a key cut to the proper length.

**Pin Tumbler Lock** - A lock using pin tumblers.

**Plug** - The part of a cylinder lock which contains the key way and turns when the tumblers are properly aligned by the key.

**Push Key** - Lines up each lever by pushing straight in without rotation.

**Shackle** - The curved part of a lock that swings to one side and fits through a staple.

**Stop** - A word often used in place of "dog".

**Tumblers** - Either pin, wafer, lever or disc, each of a different design used to prevent the lock from opening without the proper key.

**Wafer Tumbler** - A flat piece of brass with a hole in the center and a spring on the side to keep it in the extended position when the key is inserted into the center hole. The spring causes the tumbler to drop to the bottom of the cut, thus lining it up with the top of the plug.

**Ward** - An obstruction which prevents a blank or wrong key from turning in a lock.

**Warded Lock** - Locks having no movable tumblers. Such a lock is called a ward lock.

# Lock Facts

The following factors were taken into consideration when establishing lock values; rarity, condition, manufacturer and construction.

**Copper alloy locks** (brass or bronze)
Generally dictate a higher value than steel or iron ones.

**Padlock keys**
Generally the price of a lock does not depend on whether original keys are with it. One exception to the rule is railroad locks. When the original key is with it add five dollars or more to the value. These keys usually are stamped with the initials of the railroad.

**Some types of locks that can increase in value**
Railroad locks
Worlds Fair locks
Advertising locks if embossed with name of advertiser
Winchesters, Keen Cutter and etc...

Lock keys of all types and sizes are collectible especially if they are brass or bronze but beware of reproductions. Locks made of brass or bronze are attractive when cleaned or polished but generally will appeal to a collector more if left uncleaned with normal wear or patina.

It is my estimation that few older American made locks are being reproduced. Some cheap versions of the early handmade blacksmith types are around but it is not something to be concerned about at least, as of this writing. Most quality locks were made of either iron, copper, copper alloy (brass or bronze) or steel. Many locks were made of more than one metal. An example: brass body and iron hasp or vice versa. Sometimes the same locks were made of two or three different metals. Obviously this was done so that the same lock could be placed in different price categories.

Most information listed with each lock in this book is the information stamped or embossed on it. Additional information and reference came from the following books: *Professional Locksmithing and Key Making, The Manual of Locksmithing, The Padlock Code Book, The Padlock Collector.*

The collection in this book was put together for the most part in the middle west and near south. The suggested pricing comes from buying at the larger flea markets, antique shops and auctions, plus many other too numerous to mention.

# Lock Markings

The following is a list of some of the more common initials found on locks. Quite often only the initials appear.

| | | | |
|---|---|---|---|
| A & W Co. | Adams & Westlake Co. | S.B. & Co. | Slaymaker Barry Co. |
| D.M. & Co. | Davenport Mallory & Co. | S & Co. | Sargent & Co. |
| E | Eagle | S & E Co. | Smith & Egge Co. |
| F | E.T. Fraim Lock Co. | U.S. | United States Lock Co. |
| F - S | Fraim-Slaymaker Hardware Co. | W | Waterbury Lock & Specialty Co. |
| M.L. Co. | Miller Lock Co. | W & Co. | Wilcox & Co. |
| M.W. Co. | Mallory Wheeler & Co. | W.W. & Co. | William Wilcox & Co. |
| R & E Co. | Russell & Erwin Co. | Y & T | Yale & Towne Mfg. Co. |
| S | Slaymaker Lock Co. | | |

# Ward Locks
# Wrought Iron
# Early Hardware Co. Locks

*Top Row: (Left to Right)*
1. — .................................... $ 7.00-15.00
2. S & Co. ............................. 7.00-15.00
3. — .................................... 7.00-15.00
4. — .................................... 7.00-15.00

*2nd Row:*
1. MN & Co. ......................... $ 7.00-15.00
2. — .................................... 7.00-15.00
3. J & N .............................. 7.00-15.00
4. N.L.M. Co. ....................... 7.00-15.00

*3rd Row:*
1. — .................................... $ 7.00-15.00
2. — .................................... 7.00-15.00
3. — .................................... 15.00-20.00
4. — .................................... 15.00-20.00

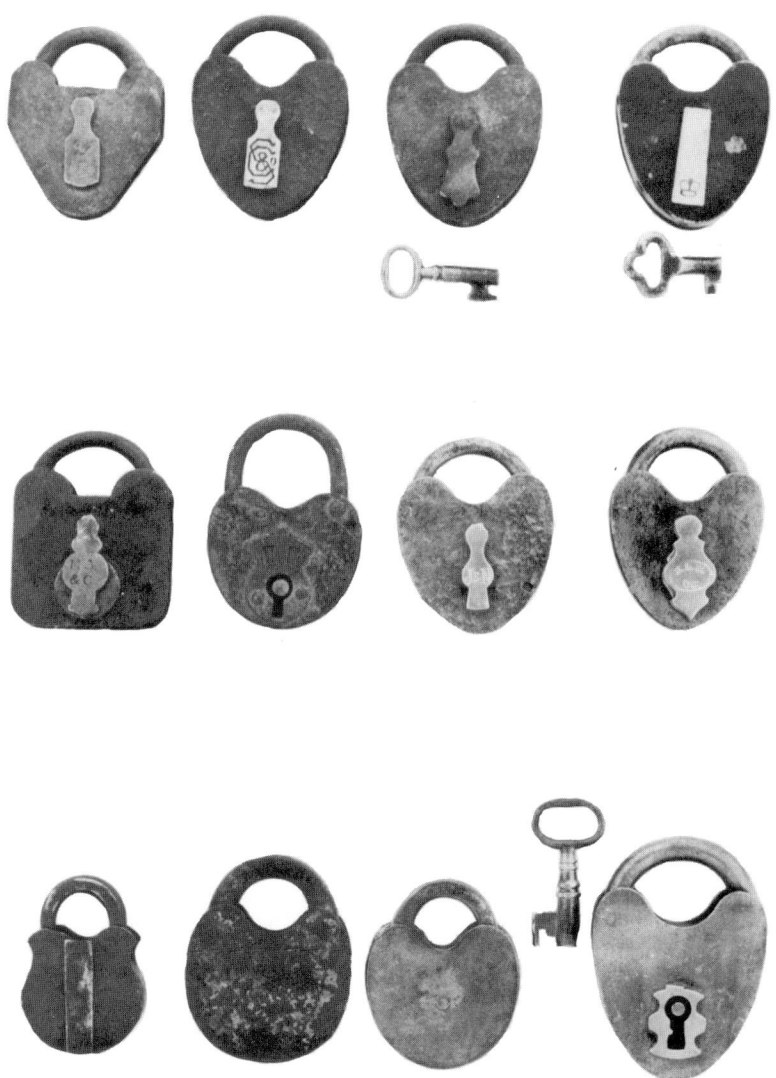

# Ward Locks
# Wrought Iron

*Top Row: (Left to Right)*
1. — .................................... $15.00-20.00
2. MW & Co. ........................... 15.00-20.00
3. MW & Co. ........................... 15.00-20.00
4. Secure Lever ....................... 15.00-20.00

*2nd Row:*
1. MW & Co. ........................... $15.00-20.00
2. VR ................................. 15.00-20.00
3. MW & Co. ........................... 15.00-20.00

*3rd Row:*
1. DM & Co. ........................... $15.00-20.00
2. MW & Co. ........................... 15.00-20.00
3. VR ................................. 15.00-20.00

# Ward Locks
# Wrought Iron

*Top Row: (Left to Right)*
1. — ................................. $15.00-20.00
2. — ................................. 15.00-20.00
3. N.H. & Co. ....................... 15.00-20.00
4. W & Co. .......................... 15.00-20.00

*2nd Row:*
1. — ................................. $15.00-20.00
2. — ................................. 15.00-20.00
3. — ................................. 15.00-20.00

*3rd Row:*
1. — ................................. $15.00-20.00
2. — ................................. 15.00-20.00
3. — ................................. 15.00-20.00

# Ward Locks
# Wrought Iron

*Top Row: (Left to Right)*
1. —  ................................. $20.00-25.00
2. MW & Co. ......................... 20.00-25.00
3. MW & Co. ......................... 20.00-25.00
4. —  ................................. 20.00-25.00

*2nd Row:*
1. MW & Co. ......................... $20.00-25.00
2. English VR ....................... 25.00-35.00
3. MW & Co. ......................... 25.00-35.00

*3rd Row:*
1. DM & Co. ......................... $25.00-35.00
2. MW & Co. ......................... 25.00-35.00
3. English VR ....................... 25.00-35.00

# Ward Locks

*Top Row: (Left to Right)*
1. Royal .............................. $4.00-5.00
2. Reese ............................. 4.00-5.00
3. Slaymaker ........................ 4.00-5.00
4. Reese ............................. 4.00-5.00
5. Super-Loc ........................ 4.00-5.00

*2nd Row:*
1. Gold Seal ........................ $4.00-5.00
2. Safeguard ........................ 4.00-5.00
3. Slaymaker ........................ 4.00-5.00
4. Acme ............................. 4.00-5.00
5. Fraim ............................ 4.00-5.00

*3rd Row:*
1. — ................................ $4.00-5.00
2. IMP .............................. 4.00-5.00
3. Star ............................. 4.00-5.00
4. Fraim-Slaymaker .................. 4.00-5.00
5. Conqueror ........................ 4.00-5.00

*4th Row:*
1. Miller; Enders ................... $4.00-5.00
2. Reese ............................ 4.00-5.00
3. Edwards .......................... 4.00-5.00
4. Pyrofax Gas Service .............. 4.00-5.00
5. Victory .......................... 4.00-5.00

   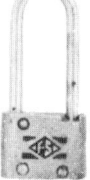 

# Ward Locks

*Top Row: (Left to Right)*
1. Fraim; Ace ............................ $6.00- 7.00
2. Fraim ................................ 7.00-15.00
3. Fraim; Mail RFD .................... 5.00- 6.00
4. Fraim Slaymaker .................... 5.00- 6.00

*2nd Row:*
1. Giant Lever ......................... $5.00- 6.00
2. Climax .............................. 7.00-15.00
3. Yale; Jr. Vulcan .................... 6.00- 7.00
4. Reese; Auto-Lock ................... 6.00- 7.00

*3rd Row:*
1. Miller; William Enders Oak Leaf ....... $6.00- 7.00
2. Corbin .............................. 4.00- 5.00

*4th Row:*
1. Slaymaker .......................... 6.00- 7.00
2. Fraim; Belknap 47 ................... 6.00- 7.00
3. Amco ............................... 4.00- 5.00
4. — ................................ 5.00- 6.00

# Ward Locks

*Top Row: (Left to Right)*
1. Corbin .................................. $6.00- 7.00
2. Slaymaker ............................. 2.00- 3.00
3. — ....................................... 1.00- 2.00
4. Foxboro Co. .......................... 6.00- 7.00
5. Slaymaker ............................. 5.00- 6.00

*2nd Row:*
1. Fraim Slaymaker; Mail RFD ........... $6.00- 7.00
2. Fraim Slaymaker; 1902 Guard ......... 6.00- 7.00
3. Slaymaker; RFD ...................... 6.00- 7.00
4. Fraim; Victory ....................... 6.00- 7.00
5. Segal ................................... 5.00- 6.00

*3rd Row:*
1. Safe .................................... $5.00- 6.00
2. Simmons .............................. 6.00- 7.00
3. Chicago Lock Co.; King ............. 6.00- 7.00
4. Reese .................................. 6.99- 7.00
5. — ....................................... 6.00- 7.00

*4th Row:*
1. Shapleigh ............................. $6.00- 7.00
2. — ....................................... 6.00- 7.00
3. Bulls Eye ............................. 7.00-15.00
4. Eagle .................................. 7.00-15.00
5. Eagle .................................. 6.00- 7.00

    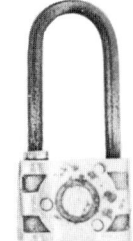

# Ward Locks

*Top Row: (Left to Right)*
1. Military Gun Rack Lock; "Screw Key";
   US .................................. $25.00-35.00
2. Eagle ............................. 7.00-15.00
3. Sterling; Sterling Jr. ................. 6.00- 7.00
4. Sterling ............................ 25.00-35.00

*2nd Row:*
1. — .................................. $15.00-20.00
2. Fraim; Secure ...................... 4.00- 5.00
3. Master; (Not Ward - Pin Tumbler) ..... 6.00- 7.00
4. — .................................. 7.00-15.00

*3rd Row:*
1. — .................................. $35.00 & up
2. Fraim Slaymaker; J.C. Higgins ........ 6.00- 7.00
3. Wayne ............................. 6.00- 7.00

*4th Row:*
1. Kabulock .......................... $15.00-20.00
2. Yale; Simmons ..................... 7.00-15.00
3. Fraim ............................. 7.00-15.00
4. Eagle ............................. 7.00-15.00

# Ward Locks

*Top Row: (Left to Right)*
1. Fraim Slaymaker; Victory .............. $7.00-15.00
2. Slaymaker ........................ 6.00- 7.00
3. Slaymaker; Flash .................. 7.00-15.00
4. Slaymaker ........................ 7.00-15.00
5. Slaymaker; Excel .................. 7.00-15.00

*2nd Row:*
1. Slaymaker; Safety First ............. $7.00-15.00
2. Slaymaker; Old Glory ............... 7.00-15.00
3. Eagle ............................ 6.00- 7.00
4. Record .......................... 6.00- 7.00

*3rd Row:*
1. Lucky ........................... $6.00- 7.00
2. Fraim Slaymaker .................. 6.00- 7.00
3. Realoc .......................... 6.00- 7.00
4. Seal ............................ 6.00- 7.00

*4th Row:*
1. Keystone ........................ $6.00- 7.00
2. Jewel ........................... 6.00- 7.00
3. Fraim Slaymaker .................. 6.00- 7.00
4. Miller ........................... 4.00- 5.00

# Ward Locks

*Top Row: (Left to Right)*
1. J.M.V & Co. .......................... $25.00-35.00
2. Fraim; Fordloc ...................... 20.00-25.00
3. — ................................. 20.00-25.00
4. — ................................. 6.00- 7.00

*2nd Row:*
1. Miller ............................. $25.00-35.00
2. Safe ............................... 5.00- 6.00
3. Miller; Protector Jr. ................ 6.00- 7.00
4. Eagle .............................. 7.00-15.00

*3rd Row:*
1. Eagle .............................. $ 5.00- 6.00
2. Corbin ............................. 5.00- 6.00
3. 6-Lever ............................ 3.00- 4.00
4. Fraim .............................. 6.00- 7.00

*4th Row:*
1. Belknap Bluegrass ................... $ 6.00- 7.00
2. Eagle .............................. 6.00- 7.00
3. Eagle .............................. 6.00- 7.00
4. Simmons - Preparedness .............. 6.00- 7.00

# Ward Locks

*Top Row: (Left to Right)*
1. Briggs & Stratton; Diamond .......... $15.00-20.00
2. Automatic ......................... 15.00-20.00
3. Unique ............................ 6.00- 7.00
4. Fraim; US Army .................... 15.00-20.00

*2nd Row:*
1. Crescent .......................... $15.00-20.00
2. Winall US ......................... 6.00- 7.00
3. Star .............................. 6.00- 7.00
4. — ................................ 5.00- 6.00

*3rd Row:*
1. — ................................ $ 5.00- 6.00
2. G & B Mfg. Co. .................... 5.00- 6.00
3. Winchester ........................ 35.00 & up
4. — ................................ 4.00- 5.00

*4th Row:*
1. — ................................ $ 4.00- 5.00
2. Sargent ........................... 6.00- 7.00
3. Edwards ........................... 5.00- 6.00
4. Yale; Miller ...................... 15.00-20.00
5. Yale; Miller ...................... 15.00-20.00

  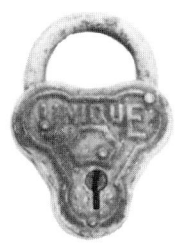 

# Ward Locks

*Top Row: (Left to Right)*
1. M.W. & Co. .............................. $15.00-20.00
2. D.M. & Co. .............................. 15.00-20.00
3. M.W. & Co. .............................. 15.00-20.00
4. M.W. & Co. .............................. 15.00-20.00
5. — ....................................... 15.00-20.00
6. — ....................................... 15.00-20.00
7. M.W. & Co. .............................. 15.00-20.00

*2nd Row:*
1. W.W. Mfg. ............................... $15.00-20.00
2. — ....................................... 6.00- 7.00
3. Corbin .................................. 6.00- 7.00
4. Corbin .................................. 6.00- 7.00
5. — ....................................... 6.00- 7.00
6. Reese ................................... 6.00- 7.00
7. Bristol ................................. 6.00- 7.00
8. — ....................................... 6.00- 7.00

*3rd Row:*
1. Brown ................................... $ 6.00- 7.00
2. Eagle ................................... 2.00- 3.00
3. — ....................................... 2.00- 3.00
4. — ....................................... 2.00- 3.00
5. — ....................................... 2.00- 3.00
6. Grammes ................................. 2.00- 3.00
7. — ....................................... 2.00- 3.00
8. — ....................................... 2.00- 3.00
9. Bison ................................... 2.00- 3.00
10. — ...................................... 2.00- 3.00

*4th Row:*
1. Eagle; Eureka ........................... $ 7.00-15.00
2. Eagle; Eureka ........................... 7.00-15.00
3. Eagle; Eureka ........................... 7.00-15.00
4. Eagle ................................... 7.00-15.00
5. Corbin; Gem ............................. 7.00-15.00
6. Corbin; Gem ............................. 7.00-15.00

# Ward Locks

*Top Row: (Left to Right)*
1. Deluxe .............................. $3.00- 4.00
2. Eagle; Pilot ........................ 3.00- 4.00
3. Belknap Bluegrass ................... 5.00- 6.00
4. Rust Proofed ........................ 5.00- 6.00

*2nd Row:*
1. Armor .............................. $5.00- 6.00
2. Shurloc ............................. 5.00- 6.00
3. Lion ................................ 5.00- 6.00
4. Fraim ............................... 5.00- 6.00
5. Dock ................................ 6.00- 7.00

*3rd Row:*
1. Belmont ............................ $6.00- 7.00
2. — ................................... 6.00- 7.00
3. St. Louis ........................... 6.00- 7.00
4. US .................................. 6.00- 7.00
5. J.W.M. .............................. 6.00- 7.00

*4th Row:*
1. — .................................. $6.00- 7.00
2. S.B. Co. ............................ 7.00-15.00
3. — ................................... 7.00-15.00
4. Penn ................................ 7.00-15.00
5. Royal ............................... 7.00-15.00

# Ward Locks

*Top Row: (Left to Right)*
1. J.H.W. Climax .................... $ 7.00-15.00
2. Russell & Erwin; Mail Box .......... 25.00-35.00
3. — ............................... 7.00-15.00
4. — ............................... 7.00-15.00

*2nd Row:*
1. — ............................... $ 7.00-15.00
2. — ............................... 7.00-15.00
3. Globe Master ...................... 6.00- 7.00
4. — ............................... 6.00- 7.00

*3rd Row:*
1. Yale ............................. $ 6.00- 7.00
2. Fraim ............................ 15.00-20.00
3. Eagle ............................ 7.00-15.00
4. — ............................... 7.00-15.00

*4th Row:*
1. Barnes; Good Luck ................. $35.00 & up
2. Barnes; Good Luck ................. 35.00 & up
3. Fraim; Keystone ................... 7.00-15.00
4. Fraim; Van Camps .................. 6.00- 7.00

# Ward Locks

*Top Row: (Left to Right)*
1. Edwards; Omeco .................... $4.00-5.00
2. Yale; Vigilant ..................... 6.00-7.00
3. Fraim; Mail ....................... 5.00-6.00
4. Fraim ............................. 3.00-4.00
5. Fraim ............................. 3.00-4.00

*2nd Row:*
1. Miller; Bulldog ................... $3.00-4.00
2. Miller ............................ 3.00-4.00
3. Eagle ............................. 3.00-4.00
4. Columbus ......................... 3.00-4.00
5. Miller; Miloco .................... 3.00-4.00
6. Eagle ............................. 3.00-4.00

*3rd Row:*
1. Eagle ............................. $3.00-4.00
2. Slaymaker ........................ 1.00-2.00
3. Slaymaker ........................ 1.00-2.00
4. Eagle ............................. 5.00-6.00
5. Yale; Yale Jr. .................... 5.00-6.00

*4th Row:*
1. Corbin ............................ $5.00-6.00
2. Corbin ............................ 5.00-6.00
3. Slaymaker ........................ 5.00-6.00
4. Yale .............................. 6.00-7.00
5. Slaymaker ........................ 5.00-6.00

    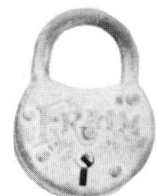

# Ward Locks

*Top Row: (Left to Right)*
1. Miller; Miloco .......................... $6.00- 7.00
2. Yale; Belknap .......................... 7.00-15.00
3. Reese .................................. 3.00- 4.00
4. Corbin; Aetna .......................... 6.00- 7.00

*2nd Row:*
1. Yale; Belknap .......................... $7.00-15.00
2. Corbin; Hercules ....................... 4.00- 5.00
3. Corbin; Hercules ....................... 4.00- 5.00
4. Yale ................................... 4.00- 5.00

*3rd Row:*
1. Fraim .................................. $4.00- 5.00
2. Climax ................................. 7.00-15.00
3. Handmade ............................... 20.00-25.00
4. Handmade, "1870" ....................... 25.00-35.00

# Ward Locks

*Top Row: (Left to Right)*
1. Fraim; Auto .......................... $15.00-20.00
2. Fraim Slaymaker; Neplus Ultra ........ 7.00-15.00
3. Eagle; Invader ..................... 7.00-15.00
4. Fraim ............................. 15.00-20.00

*2nd Row:*
1. Fraim; US Sampson ................. $ 6.00- 7.00
2. Fraim; Secure ..................... 6.00- 7.00
3. Fraim; New Era .................... 6.00- 7.00
4. Fraim; Imperial ................... 6.00- 7.00

*3rd Row:*
1. Fraim; Pequot ..................... $ 7.00-15.00
2. Yale; Cyclops ..................... 7.00-15.00
3. Yale ............................. 5.00- 6.00
4. J.S.H. & Co. ...................... 6.00- 7.00

*4th Row:*
1. Old Glory ......................... $ 6.00- 7.00
2. Stability ......................... 6.00- 7.00
3. Fraim ............................ 5.00- 6.00
4. Corbin ........................... 5.00- 6.00

# Ward Locks

*Top Row: (Left to Right)*
1. Master; Ace .......................... $4.00- 5.00
2. Reese ............................. 5.00- 6.00
3. — ................................ 7.00-15.00
4. — ................................ 4.00- 5.00

*2nd Row:*
1. Excelsior; Leader ................... $3.00- 4.00
2. Eagle ............................. 5.00- 6.00
3. Eagle ............................. 5.00- 6.00
4. Corbin; Valiant .................... 3.00-4.00

*3rd Row:*
1. Corbin; Bruno ...................... $3.00- 4.00
2. Corbin; Pyramid ................... 3.00- 4.00
3. Corbin; Van ........................ 3.00- 4.00
4. Fraim; Napolean ................... 3.00- 4.00

*4th Row:*
1. Fraim; Auto Go ..................... $3.00- 4.00
2. Fraim; King Korn .................. 3.00- 4.00
3. Fraim; Savage ...................... 3.00- 4.00
4. Eagle; Emerald .................... 5.00- 6.00

# Ward Locks

*Top Row: (Left to Right)*
1. Slaymaker .......................... $3.00- 4.00
2. Slaymaker; Convoy ................. 3.00- 4.00
3. Slaymaker; Pioneer ................. 3.00- 4.00
4. Corbin; Bull ....................... 3.00- 4.00

*2nd Row:*
1. Corbin; Radio ...................... $3.00- 4.00
2. Corbin; Radio ...................... 3.00- 4.00
3. Corbin; Beta ....................... 3.00- 4.00
4. Corbin; Vici ....................... 3.00- 4.00

*3rd Row:*
1. Eagle; Opal ........................ $3.00- 4.00
2. Miller; Rugby ...................... 3.00- 4.00
3. Eagle; Dragon ...................... 3.00- 4.00
4. Edwards; Omeco .................... 4.00- 5.00

*4th Row:*
1. Corbin; Orion ...................... $6.00- 7.00
2. Corbin; Pluto ...................... 6.00- 7.00
3. Fraim .............................. 7.00-15.00
4. Fraim .............................. 7.00-15.00

# Ward Locks

*Top Row: (Left to Right)*
1. Slaymaker; York .................... $ 6.00- 7.00
2. Wise-Lock ......................... 15.00-20.00
3. Wise-Lock ......................... 15.00-20.00
4. Fraim; New Century ................ 20.00-25.00

*2nd Row:*
1. Fraim; New Century ................ $15.00-20.00
2. S.B. Co.; Sprocket ................. 20.00-25.00
3. — ................................. 15.00-20.00
4. Reese ............................. 6.00- 7.00

*3rd Row:*
1. Miller ............................ $ 7.00-15.00
2. Fraim Slaymaker; Fordloc .......... 7.00-15.00
3. Corbin ............................ 15.00-20.00

*4th Row:*
1. Fraim; Tire-Lock .................. $ 7.00-15.00
2. German; Burg ...................... 5.00- 6.00
3. German ............................ 4.00- 5.00

  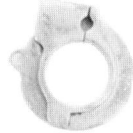 

# Ward Locks

*Top Row: (Left to Right)*
1. German .......................... $ 5.00- 6.00
2. German ..........................   6.00- 7.00

*2nd Row:*
1. German .......................... $25.00-35.00

*2nd Row:*
1. German .......................... $ 2.00- 3.00
2. German ..........................   3.00- 4.00
3. German ..........................   3.00- 4.00

# Wafer
## Scandinavian Type Jail Locks

*Top Row: (Left to Right)*
1. J.W. Climax ........................ $15.00-20.00
2. J.W. Climax ........................ 15.00-20.00
3. J.W. Climax ........................ 15.00-20.00
4. Fraim ............................. 25.00-35.00
5. Fraim ............................. 25.00-35.00

*2nd Row:*
1. Star .............................. $35.00 & up
2. Fraim ............................. 7.00-15.00
3. Fraim ............................. 7.00-15.00
4. — ................................ 7.00-15.00

*3rd Row:*
1. — ................................ $ 7.00-15.00
2. Star .............................. 20.00-25.00
3. Star .............................. 15.00-20.00

*4th Row:*
1. Star .............................. $15.00-20.00
2. Russell Erwin & Co. ................ 20.00-25.00
3. Miller; 99 ........................ 20.00-25.00
4. Burglar Stop ...................... 20.00-25.00

# Wafer Locks

*Top Row: (Left to Right)*
1. Lion .............................. $4.00- 5.00
2. — ................................ 7.00-15.00
3. Eagle; Police Pup .................. 5.00- 6.00
4. Fraim ............................. 7.00-15.00

*2nd Row:*
1. Eagle; Coop Padlock ................ $5.00- 6.00
2. Slaymaker ......................... 5.00- 6.00
3. Fraim ............................. 5.00- 6.00

*3rd Row:*
1. Fraim; True Value .................. $5.00- 6.00
2. Slaymaker: Super ................... 5.00- 6.00
3. Illinois Lock Co. ................... 3.00- 4.00

# 2 Lever Locks

*Top Row: (Left to Right)*
1. U.S. Mail ........................... $ 7.00-15.00
2. Master ............................. 3.00- 4.00
3. Yale; Y&T ......................... 25.00-35.00
4. Yale ............................... 7.00-15.00
5. Yale ............................... 6.00- 7.00

*2nd Row:*
1. Yale ............................... $ 6.00- 7.00
2. Yale ............................... 6.00- 7.00
3. Yale ............................... 7.00-15.00
4. Eagle; Double Locking .............. 3.00- 4.00
5. Fraim; Power Lever ................. 3.00- 4.00

*3rd Row:*
1. Yale ............................... $15.00-20.00
2. Yale ............................... 15.00-20.00
3. Yale ............................... 15.00-20.00
4. Yale ............................... 4.00- 5.00

  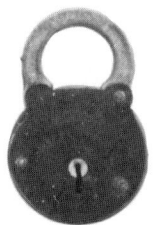 

 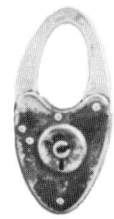  

# 2 Lever Locks

*Top Row: (Left to Right)*
1. —  .................................... $7.00-15.00
2. Corbin ............................ 7.00-15.00
3. J.H.W. ............................ 7.00-15.00
4. — .................................... 7.00-15.00

*2nd Row:*
1. Eagle ............................. $7.00-15.00
2. — .................................... 7.00-15.00
3. Cycle ............................. 7.00-15.00
4. — .................................... 7.00-15.00

*3rd Row:*
1. — .................................... $7.00-15.00
2. Eagle ............................. 7.00-15.00
3. Romer ........................... 7.00-15.00
4. Romer ........................... 7.00-15.00

*4th Row:*
1. — .................................... $7.00-15.00
2. — .................................... 7.00-15.00
3. — .................................... 7.00-15.00
4. — .................................... 7.00-15.00
5. Wheel ............................ 7.00-15.00

# 3 Lever Locks

*Top Row: (Left to Right)*
1. Master; 48 .......................... $ 7.00-15.00
2. Eagle ............................. 6.00- 7.00
3. Master ............................ 4.00- 5.00
4. Illinois Power Co. .................. 25.00-35.00

*2nd Row:*
1. — ............................... $ 6.00- 7.00
2. Yale ............................. 5.00- 6.00
3. Yale ............................. 5.00- 6.00
4. Yale ............................. 5.00- 6.00

*3rd Row:*
1. Yale ............................. $15.00-20.00
2. Yale ............................. 15.00-20.00
3. Yale ............................. 15.00-20.00
4. Yale ............................. 15.00-20.00

*4th Row:*
1. Defiance .......................... $ 6.00- 7.00
2. Russell & Erwin; Guardian ........... 6.00- 7.00
3. Miller; Protector ................... 6.00- 7.00
4. Eagle ............................. 6.00- 7.00

# 3 Lever Locks

*Top Row: (Left to Right)*
1. Yale ................................. $25.00-35.00
2. Corbin ............................ 7.00-15.00
3. — ................................... 6.00- 7.00
4. Eagle ............................. 20.00-25.00

*2nd Row:*
1. Eagle ............................. $ 5.00- 6.00
2. Ten Star ......................... 15.00-20.00
3. Fraim; Winchester ........ 35.00 & up
4. Yale .............................. 20.00-25.00

*3rd Row:*
1. Sargent .......................... $15.00-20.00
2. Corbin ........................... 15.00-20.00
3. Corbin ........................... 15.00-20.00
4. Corbin ........................... 15.00-20.00

*4th Row:*
1. Corbin ........................... $20.00-25.00
2. Eagle ............................. 5.00- 6.00
3. Eagle ............................. 7.00-15.00
4. Tiny .............................. 5.00- 6.00
5. Columbus ..................... 5.00- 6.00

# 3 Lever Locks

*Top Row: (Left to Right)*
1. Wilson Bohannon ................... $25.00-35.00
2. Wilson Bohannon ................... 25.00-35.00
3. Wilson Bohannon ................... 25.00-35.00
4. Simmons Keen Kutter ............... 35.00 & up
5. Miller ............................ 7.00-15.00

*2nd Row:*
1. Sargent ........................... $ 7.00-15.00
2. Reese; Chief ...................... 7.00-15.00
3. Fraim; Simmons .................... 15.00-20.00
4. Reese ............................. 7.00-15.00

*3rd Row:*
1. Fraim ............................. $ 7.00-15.00
2. Eagle ............................. 7.00-15.00
3. Eagle ............................. 7.00-15.00
4. Fraim; Pogoma ..................... 15.00-20.00

*4th Row:*
1. Yale .............................. $ 7.00-15.00
2. Fraim; Anchor ..................... 7.00-15.00
3. Corbin ............................ 7.00-15.00

  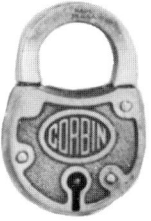

# 4 Lever Locks

*Top Row: (Left to Right)*
1. Corbin .............................. $20.00-25.00
2. Yale ............................... 7.00-15.00
3. Eagle .............................. 15.00-20.00
4. Yale; Belknap ...................... 25.00-35.00

*2nd Row:*
1. Fraim; D.E. Co. .................... $25.00-35.00
2. Yale ............................... 25.00-35.00
3. Eagle .............................. 7.00-15.00
4. Wilson Bohannon; U.S. Gov't. Control .. 25.00-35.00

*3rd Row:*
1. Fraim; Western Union ................ $25.00-35.00
2. Yale ............................... 15.00-20.00
3. Yale ............................... 15.00-20.00

*4th Row:*
1. Locking Chain Corp; Trio Chain Lock .. $ 7.00-15.00
2. Board of Education ................. 25.00-35.00
3. Yale ............................... 35.00 & up

# 4 Lever Railroad Pin Tumbler Locks

*Top Row: (Left to Right)*
1. Slaymaker; A.T. & S.F. .............. $20.00-25.00
2. Raco ............................... 15.00-20.00
3. Illinois Central Signal .............. 7.00-15.00
4. Fraim; Penn. Railroad .............. 20.00-25.00

*2nd Row:*
1. Yale; L & N ........................ $20.00-25.00
2. Xmplr; N.C. & St. Louis ............ 15.00-20.00
3. Corbin; N.Y. Railway - Moon ........ 20.00-25.00
4. Yale; Southern Railway ............. 15.00-20.00

*3rd Row:*
1. Fraim; I.C.R.R. .................... $20.00-25.00
2. Fraim; I.C.R.R. .................... 20.00-25.00
3. Yale; Southern Railway ............. 20.00-25.00

# 4 Lever Railroad Pin Tumbler Locks

*Top Row: (Left to Right)*
1. Fraim; D.L. & W. Railway ............. $25.00-35.00
2. Slaymaker; P.C. Railway .............. 25.00-35.00
3. William Bohannon; M&O Railroad ..... 25.00-35.00
4. Slaymaker; Pan Handle Railroad ....... 25.00-35.00

*2nd Row:*
1. William Bohannon; MK & T Railroad .. $25.00-35.00
2. Corbin; L & N ...................... 20.00-25.00
3. Yale; P.C.T. Railroad ............... 25.00-35.00
4. Santa Fe ........................... 35.00 & up

*3rd Row:*
1. L & N Railroad ..................... $25.00-35.00
2. Corbin; B & O Railroad .............. 20.00-25.00
3. Slaymaker; St. Louis & San Francisco R.R. ............................ 25.00-35.00
4. Yale; B & O Signal .................. 20.00-25.00

# 4 Lever, 5 Lever, 6 Lever Push Key Railroad Pin Tumbler Locks

*Top Row: (Left to Right)*
1. Simmons Keen Kutter; Santa Fe ....... $35.00 & up
2. L & N .............................. 25.00-35.00
3. ICRR ............................... 25.00-35.00
4. CCC & St. Louis .................... 25.00-35.00

*2nd Row:*
1. Wilson Bohannon; N & W ............. $25.00-35.00
2. Illinois Central Signal ............ 20.00-25.00
3. AM. EX. Co. ....................... 7.00-15.00
4. Eagle; L & N ...................... 20.00-25.00

*3rd Row:*
1. Yale; GNRR ........................ $15.00-20.00
2. Corbin; NC & St. Louis Signal ..... 20.00-25.00
3. Miller; NC & St. Louis ............ 20.00-25.00
4. A & W; CCC & St. Louis ............ 25.00-35.00

*4th Row:*
1. Yale; CCC & St. Louis Signal ...... $20.00-25.00
2. E & OV ............................ 25.00-35.00
3. Slaymaker; L & N .................. 7.00-15.00

# 6 Lever Locks

*Top Row: (Left to Right)*
1. Eagle .............................. $15.00-20.00
2. Slaymaker; Steel State ............... 6.00- 7.00
3. Slaymaker; Steel State ............... 6.00- 7.00
4. Corbin; Excelsior .................... 6.00- 7.00

*2nd Row:*
1. 6 Lever ............................ $ 6.00- 7.00
2. Eagle; Salesman Sample ............. 25.00-35.00
3. Street Letter Box Lock .............. 7.00-15.00
4. Corbin; Midget ..................... 15.00-20.00

*3rd Row:*
1. Simmons Keen Kutter ................ $35.00 & up
2. Simmons Keen Kutter ................ 35.00 & up
3. Simmons Keen Kutter ................ 35.00 & up

*4th Row:*
1. Simmons Keen Kutter ................ $35.00 & up
2. Eagle .............................. 25.00-35.00
3. Eagle .............................. 25.00-35.00

# 6 Lever Locks

*Top Row: (Left to Right)*
1. Miller; Secure Lever .................. $15.00-20.00
2. Slaymaker; Standard ................ 6.00- 7.00
3. Slaymaker; 6 Lever .................. 6.00- 7.00
4. Miller; 6 Levers ..................... 6.00- 7.00

*2nd Row:*
1. Sargent ............................. $ 6.00- 7.00
2. Fraim .............................. 6.00- 7.00
3. Fraim .............................. 6.00- 7.00
4. Miller ............................. 6.00- 7.00

*3rd Row:*
1. Miller ............................. $ 6.00- 7.00
2. Miller; William Enders Oak Leaf ....... 6.00- 7.00
3. Edwards; Omeco .................... 6.00- 7.00
4. Edwards; Safety Lever ................ 6.00- 7.00

*4th Row:*
1. Miller; Simmons Quality .............. $ 6.00- 7.00
2. Corbin; Iron Clad ................... 6.00- 7.00
3. Corbin; Iron Clad ................... 6.00- 7.00
4. Corbin; Iron Side ................... 6.00- 7.00

## 6 Lever Locks

*Top Row: (Left to Right)*
1. Eagle; Winchester .................... $25.00-35.00
2. Eagle ............................... 6.00- 7.00
3. Eagle; Belknap ...................... 7.00-15.00
4. Eagle; William Enders Oak Leaf ....... 7.00-15.00

*2nd Row:*
1. Yale ............................... $ 6.00- 7.00
2. J.H.W. Climax ...................... 20.00-25.00
3. Ames Sword; 6 Lever ................. 25.00-35.00
4. Edwards ............................ 6.00- 7.00

*3rd Row:*
1. Ames Sword; 3 Lever ................. $20.00-25.00
2. Ames Sword; 2 Lever ................. 15.00-20.00
3. Sargent - Green Leaf ................ 20.00-25.00
4. Miller; New Champion ................ 6.00- 7.00

*4th Row:*
1. Yale ............................... $15.00-20.00
2. Sargent - Greenleaf .................. 20.00-25.00
3. Sargent - Greenleaf .................. 20.00-25.00
4. Eagle ............................... 7.00-15.00

# 6 Lever Locks

*Top Row: (Left to Right)*
1. Miller .............................. $15.00-20.00
2. Sargent; Simmons Wireless ............ 15.00-20.00
3. Wilson Bohannon ..................... 20.00-25.00

*2nd Row:*
1. Miller; Automatic .................... $ 6.00- 7.00
2. Eagle .............................. 7.00-15.00
3. Fraim ............................. 7.00-15.00

*3rd Row:*
1. Fraim ............................. $15.00-20.00
2. Safe .............................. 20.00-25.00
3. Safe .............................. 20.00-25.00

# 6 Lever
## Pancake Push Key Locks

*Top Row: (Left to Right)*
1. Eagle; Favorite .................... $15.00-20.00
2. Fraim; Empire ..................... 15.00-20.00
3. Miller; Belknaps ................... 15.00-20.00

*2nd Row:*
1. Climax ............................ $20.00-25.00
2. Fraim; Liberty ..................... 15.00-20.00
3. Fraim; Diamond .................... 15.00-20.00

*3rd Row:*
1. Fraim; Columbia ................... $15.00-20.00
2. Fraim; Keystone .................... 15.00-20.00
3. Miller; Champion ................... 15.00-20.00
4. Miller; Champion ................... 15.00-20.00

*4th Row:*
1. Corbin; Excelsior ................... $15.00-20.00
2. Safe; 4 Lever ....................... 20.00-25.00
3. Safe; 6 Lever ....................... 20.00-25.00
4. Fraim; Harvard .................... 15.00-20.00

# 8 Lever Locks

*Top Row: (Left to Right)*
1. Blue Chief .......................... $ 7.00-15.00
2. Mallory Wheeler; M.W. Co. ........... 7.00-15.00
3. Eagle; Mastodon ..................... 7.00-15.00
4. Safe; 8 Lever ....................... 20.00-25.00

*2nd Row:*
1. Reese ............................... $ 7.00-15.00
2. Sargent ............................. 7.00-15.00
3. Corbin; Samson ...................... 7.00-15.00
4. Eagle; Goliath ...................... 7.00-15.00

*3rd Row:*
1. Delamater Rustless .................. $ 7.00-15.00
2. Edwards ............................. 7.00-15.00
3. Slaymaker; Steel State .............. 7.00-15.00
4. Cleveland 4-Way; 8 Lever Tumbler .... 15.00-20.00

# Pin Tumbler Push Key Locks

*Top Row: (Left to Right)*
1. Yale .............................. $ 7.00-15.00
2. Corbin ........................... 7.00-15.00
3. Corbin ........................... 6.00- 7.00

*2nd Row:*
1. Yale; Lakeside ..................... $15.00-20.00
2. Eagle; Hibbard .................... 20.00-25.00
3. Eagle ............................ 7.00-15.00

*3rd Row:*
1. Eagle ............................ $15.00-20.00
2. Eagle ............................ 15.00-20.00
3. Yale ............................. 7.00-15.00
4. Fraim Slaymaker; Blue Grass BG 44 .... 15.00-20.00

*4th Row:*
1. Fraim Slaymaker; BG Bluegrass ....... $15.00-20.00
2. Fraim Slaymaker; GW & H Hercules .... 15.00-20.00
3. Fraim Slaymaker; Orgill Bros. & Co. .... 25.00-35.00
4. Yale ............................. 7.00-15.00

# Pin Tumbler Push Key Locks

*Top Row: (Left to Right)*
1. Fraim Slaymaker; Winchester ......... $35.00 & up
2. Fraim Slaymaker ................... 15.00-20.00
3. Sargent; Simmons .................. 20.00-25.00

*2nd Row:*
1. Sargent; G & W Hardware Hercules .... $15.00-20.00
2. Sargent; Simmons .................. 15.00-20.00
3. Sargent ........................... 7.00-15.00

*3rd Row:*
1. Sargent ........................... $ 7.00-15.00
2. Yale .............................. 6.00- 7.00
3. Yale; US .......................... 20.00-25.00
4. Yale; USN ......................... 20.00-25.00

*4th Row:*
1. Corbin; USMC ...................... $20.00-25.00
2. Yale .............................. 15.00-20.00
3. Yale .............................. 15.00-20.00
4. Yale .............................. 6.00- 7.00

# Pin Tumbler Locks

*Top Row: (Left to Right)*
1. Corbin ............................. $7.00-15.00
2. Corbin ............................. 7.00-15.00
3. Corbin ............................. 7.00-15.00
4. Corbin ............................. 7.00-15.00
5. Corbin ............................. 7.00-15.00

*2nd Row:*
1. Yale ............................... $7.00-15.00
2. Sargent ........................... 7.00-15.00
3. Master ............................ 7.00-15.00
4. Eagle ............................. 7.00-15.00

*3rd Row:*
1. Wilson Bohannon .................. $7.00-15.00
2. Sargent ........................... 7.00-15.00
3. Fraim ............................. 7.00-15.00
4. Eagle ............................. 7.00-15.00

*4th Row:*
1. Wilson Bohannon; IR Co. .............. $7.00-15.00
2. Best; S.O. Co. ...................... 7.00-15.00
3. Corbin; S.O. Co. .................... 7.00-15.00
4. Eagle; Standard Oil Co. ............. 7.00-15.00

# Pin Tumbler Locks

*Top Row: (Left to Right)*
1. Reese; USN .......................... $ 7.00-15.00
2. American; US ...................... 7.00-15.00
3. Fraim; USN ........................ 7.00-15.00
4. Corbin; Ordinance Dept. ............. 7.00-15.00
5. Independent Lock Co.; US ............ 7.00-15.00

*2nd Row:*
1. American ........................... $ 7.00-15.00
2. Eagle .............................. 4.00- 5.00
3. Eagle .............................. 20.00-25.00
4. Yale ............................... 6.00- 7.00
5. Corbin; Sinclair .................... 7.00-15.00

*3rd Row:*
1. Best; Chrysler ...................... $ 7.00-15.00
2. Sargent ............................ 15.00-20.00
3. Master ............................. 5.00- 6.00
4. Yale ............................... 6.00- 7.00
5. Lion ............................... 7.00-15.00

*4th Row:*
1. Eagle .............................. $ 6.00- 7.00
2. Eagle .............................. 6.00- 7.00
3. Corbin ............................. 6.00- 7.00
4. Corbin ............................. 6.00- 7.00
5. Eagle .............................. 6.00- 7.00

# Pin Tumbler Locks

*Top Row: (Left to Right)*
1. Segal .............................. $25.00-35.00
2. Segal .............................. 25.00-35.00
3. Segal .............................. 25.00-35.00
4. Best; W-S ......................... 6.00- 7.00

*2nd Row:*
1. Yale ............................... $ 4.00- 5.00
2. Ellis Bros.; Ellis Padlock .............. 6.00- 7.00
3. American .......................... 6.00- 7.00
4. Reese ............................. 6.00- 7.00

*3rd Row:*
1. Eagle ............................. $ 6.00- 7.00
2. Sargent ........................... 6.00- 7.00
3. Elgin ............................. 6.00- 7.00
4. Taylor ............................ 6.00- 7.00
5. Eagle ............................. 6.00- 7.00

*4th Row:*
1. Independent Lock Co. ............... $ 6.00- 7.00
2. Eagle ............................. 6.00- 7.00
3. Corbin ............................ 6.00- 7.00
4. Fraim ............................. 6.00- 7.00
5. Master ............................ 5.00- 6.00

# Pin Tumbler Locks

*Top Row: (Left to Right)*
1. Chicago Lock Co.; Ace .................. $ 7.00-15.00
2. Abus; Diskus, German Roll Bar ........ 15.00-20.00
3. Independent Lock Co.; Wafer ......... 7.00-15.00
4. Independent Lock Co. ................ 7.00-15.00

*2nd Row:*
1. Independent Lock Co. ................ $ 7.00-15.00
2. E.P. Hurd; Hurd Lock ............... 20.00-25.00
3. E.P. Hurd; Hurd Lock ............... 20.00-25.00
4. Yale ............................... 7.00-15.00
5. Yale ............................... 7.00-15.00

*3rd Row:*
1. Segal ............................... $15.00-20.00
2. Independent Lock Co. ................ 5.00- 6.00
3. Hurd ............................... 7.00-15.00
4. Hurd ............................... 7.00-15.00
5. Hurd ............................... 7.00-15.00

*4th Row:*
1. Hurd ............................... $ 7.00-15.00
2. Jewel Tea Co. ...................... 7.00-15.00
3. Wilson Bohannon ................... 7.00-15.00
4. Wilson Bohannon ................... 7.00-15.00
5. Wilson Bohannon ................... 7.00-15.00

# Combination Locks

*Top Row: (Left to Right)*
 1. American Keyless Lock Co.; No-Key ... $25.00-35.00
 2. American Keyless Lock Co.; No-Key ... 25.00-35.00
 3. Sesamee .......................... 6.00- 7.00
 4. — ............................... 5.00- 6.00
 5. — ............................... 5.00- 6.00

*2nd Row:*
 1. — ............................... $20.00-25.00
 2. DRP; Rollbar ..................... 5.00- 6.00
 3. Karco; German .................... 7.00-15.00
 4. Junkunc Bros. .................... 20.00-25.00

*3rd Row:*
 1. Junkunc Bros. .................... $20.00-25.00
 2. Junkunc Bros. .................... 20.00-25.00
 3. Junkunc Bros. .................... 20.00-25.00
 4. Miller ........................... 15.00-20.00

*4th Row:*
 1. US Customs ....................... $35.00 & up
 2. Miller ........................... 6.00- 7.00
 3. J.B.M.K.L. Co. ................... 6.00- 7.00
 4. Dudley ........................... 7.00-15.00
 5. Dudley ........................... 7.00-15.00

# Combination Locks

*Top Row: (Left to Right)*
1. Yale .............................. $4.00- 5.00
2. Slaymaker ........................ 4.00- 5.00
3. Slaymaker ........................ 4.00- 5.00
4. Fraim ............................ 4.00- 5.00
5. Japanese; Sports Comlock ............ 3.00- 4.00

*2nd Row:*
1. Gougler ......................... $4.00- 5.00
2. American ........................ 3.00- 4.00
3. Walsco .......................... 3.00- 4.00
4. Slaymaker ....................... 3.00- 4.00

*3rd Row:*
1. Slaymaker ....................... $3.00- 4.00
2. — ............................... 3.00- 4.00
3. — ............................... 4.00- 5.00

*4th Row:*
1. Master .......................... $6.00- 7.00
2. Master .......................... 6.00- 7.00
3. Steen Lock-Trible ................. 7.00-15.00
4. Master; Champ .................... 4.00- 5.00

# Vehicle Locks

*Top Row: (Left to Right)*
1. Lever Buckle Co.; Tourist Trunk Stap .. $15.00-20.00
2. Fox Auto Co.; Ward ................. 7.00-15.00

*2nd Row:*
1. Junkunc Bros.; Tire Lock, Grip Tumbler $35.00 & up
2. Fish Pot; Motorcycle ................ 35.00 & up

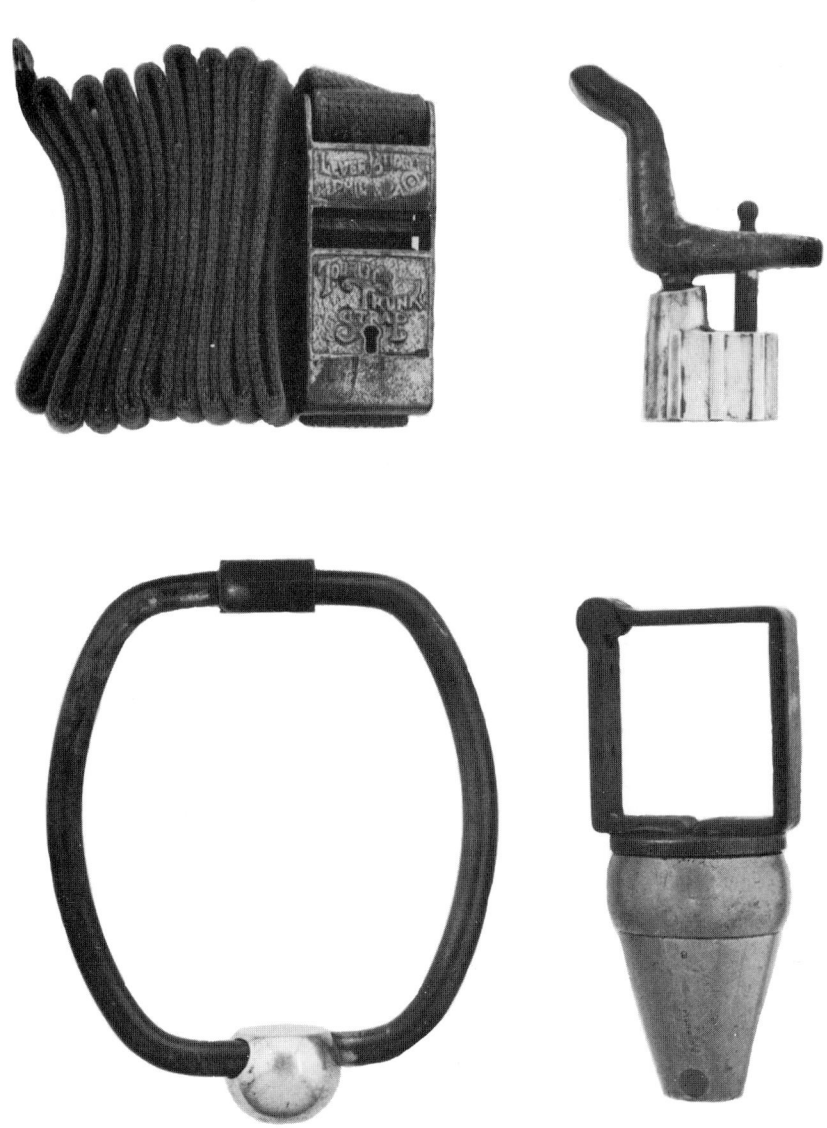

# Vehicle Locks

Corbin; Pin Tumbler, Tire Lock .......... $35.00 & up

# Vehicle Locks

Yale; Johnson Universal Spare Tire Lock,
Pin Tumbler ............................. $35.00 & up

## Jail Lock
## Safe Lock

*Top:*
    Jail Lock .............................. $25.00-35.00
*Bottom:*
    Yale Safe Lock ........................ $35.00 & up

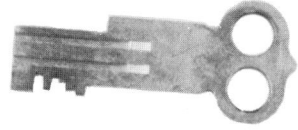

# Early Blacksmith Type Screw Key Locks

*Top Row:*
   Original .............................. $25.00-35.00
*2nd Row:*
   Original .............................. $25.00-35.00
*3rd Row:*
   Mexican Reproduction ................. $ 6.00- 7.00
*4th Row:*
   Mexican Reproduction ................. $ 6.00- 7.00

# Oriental Locks

*Top Row:*
  India .............................. $15.00-20.00
*2nd Row:*
  Chinese ............................ $20.00-25.00
*3rd Row:*
  Chinese ............................ $20.00-25.00
*4th Row:*
  Chinese ............................ $20.00-25.00

Oriental and Asian locks are generally known as Chinese locks and are common in the United States. Tourists often bring them back from China as curios. These locks come in different sizes and are generally made of brass. Some use a straight key with grooves in the sides, the springs then follow the grooves and are compressed as the key enters. The tip of the key enters the key hole first and then the handle is tipped up into a horizontal position and pushed into the lock. The square hole in the end of the key compresses the four springs towards the center of the shaft upon which they are rivited. When the key strikes the stop, it pushes the bolt out of the lock far enough to remove it.

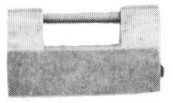

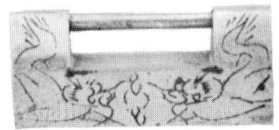

# Worlds Fair Locks

*Top Row: (Left to Right)*
1. Fraim; Front is Missouri State Seal, Back
   is embossed with St. Louis skyline ...... $25.00-35.00
2. Fraim; Raven, 1904 .................. 25.00-35.00

*Bottom Row:*
1. Panama Pacific Exposition - 1915 ....... $35.00 & up
2. Eagle; Worlds Fair 1904 .............. 35.00 & up

# Bank Vault Time Lock

Yale .................................... $350.00 & up